Dr. Hajar Dauleh

Understanding My Type 1 Diabetes

Bumblebee Books

BUMBLEBEE PAPERBACK EDITION

Copyright © Dr. Hajar Dauleh 2024

The right of Dr. Hajar Dauleh to be identified as author of
this work has been asserted in accordance with sections 77 and 78 of the
Copyright, Designs and Patents Act 1988.

All Rights Reserved

No reproduction, copy or transmission of this publication
may be made without written permission.
No paragraph of this publication may be reproduced,
copied or transmitted save with the written permission of the publisher, or in
accordance with the provisions of the Copyright Act 1956 (as amended).

Any person who commits any unauthorised act in relation to
this publication may be liable to criminal
prosecution and civil claims for damage.

A CIP catalogue record for this title is
available from the British Library.

ISBN: 978-1-78796-120-3

Bumblebee Books is an imprint of
Olympia Publishers.

First Published in 2024

Olympia Publishers
Tallis House
2 Tallis Street
London
EC4Y 0AB

Printed in Great Britain

Dedication

To all the brave young warriors living with diabetes, your strength and courage inspire us every day. This book is dedicated to you. Keep shining, keep fighting.

Human Digestive System

"Are ready? I will pour the water now."

- Mouth
- Stomach
- Intestine

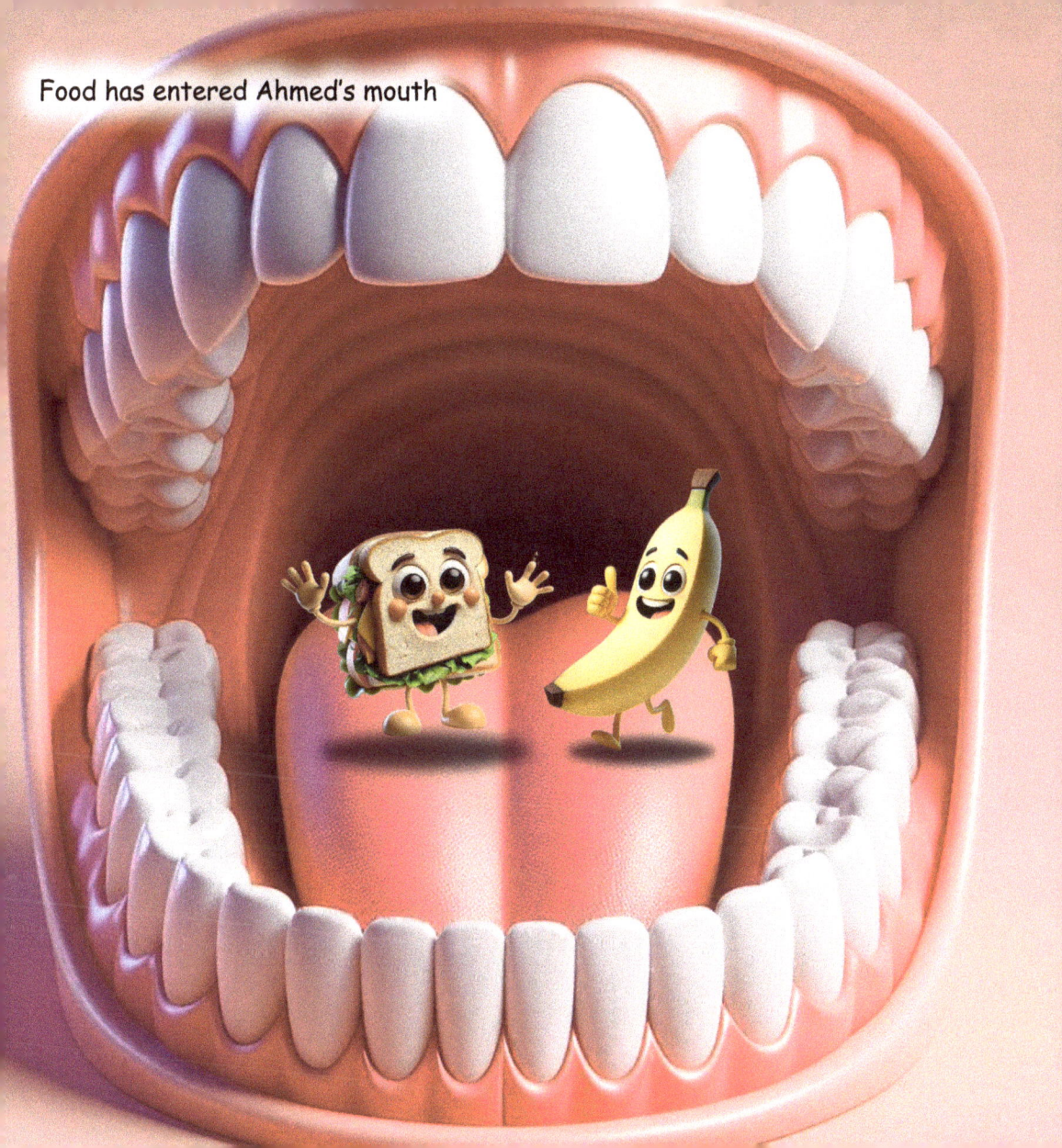

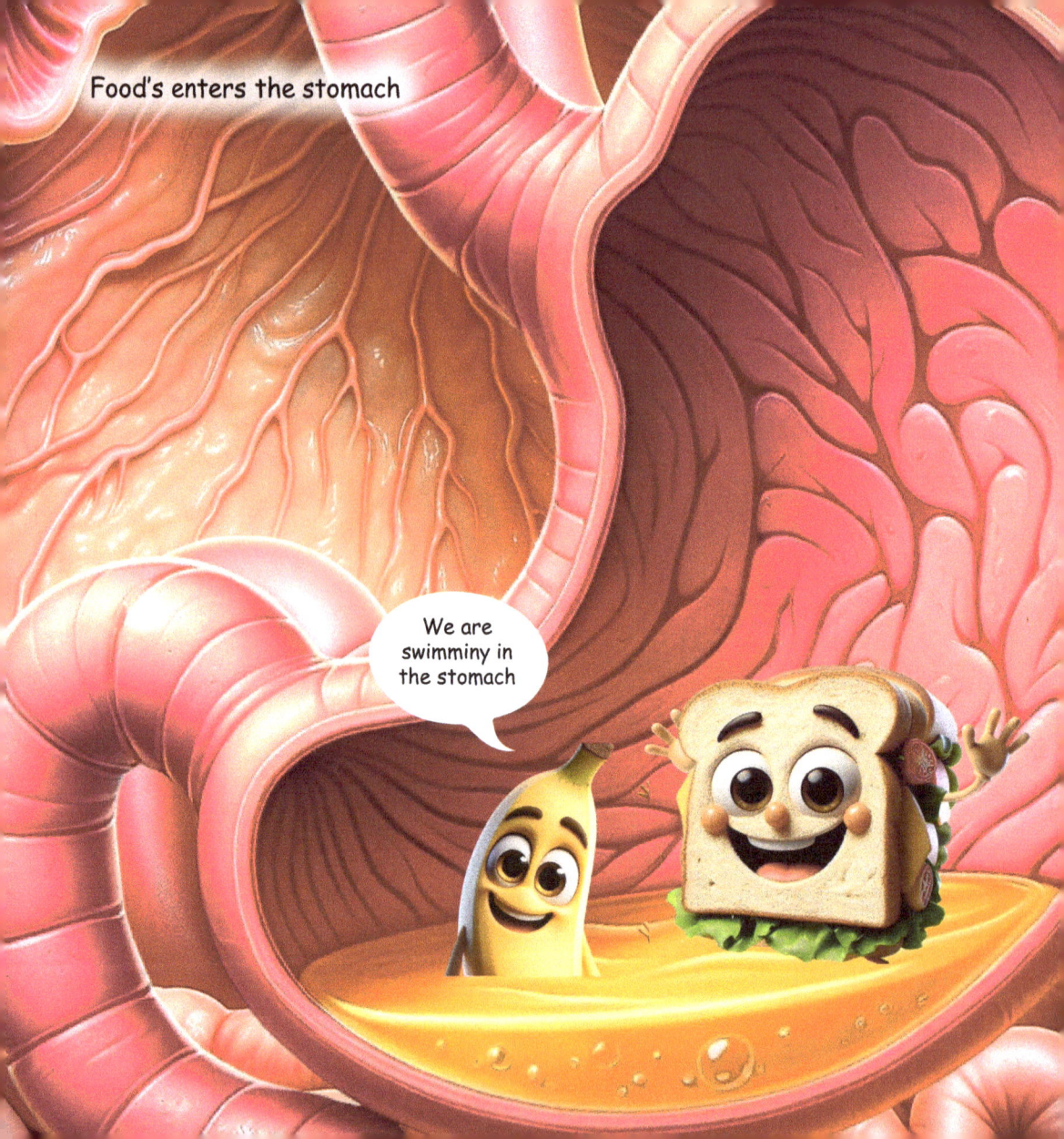

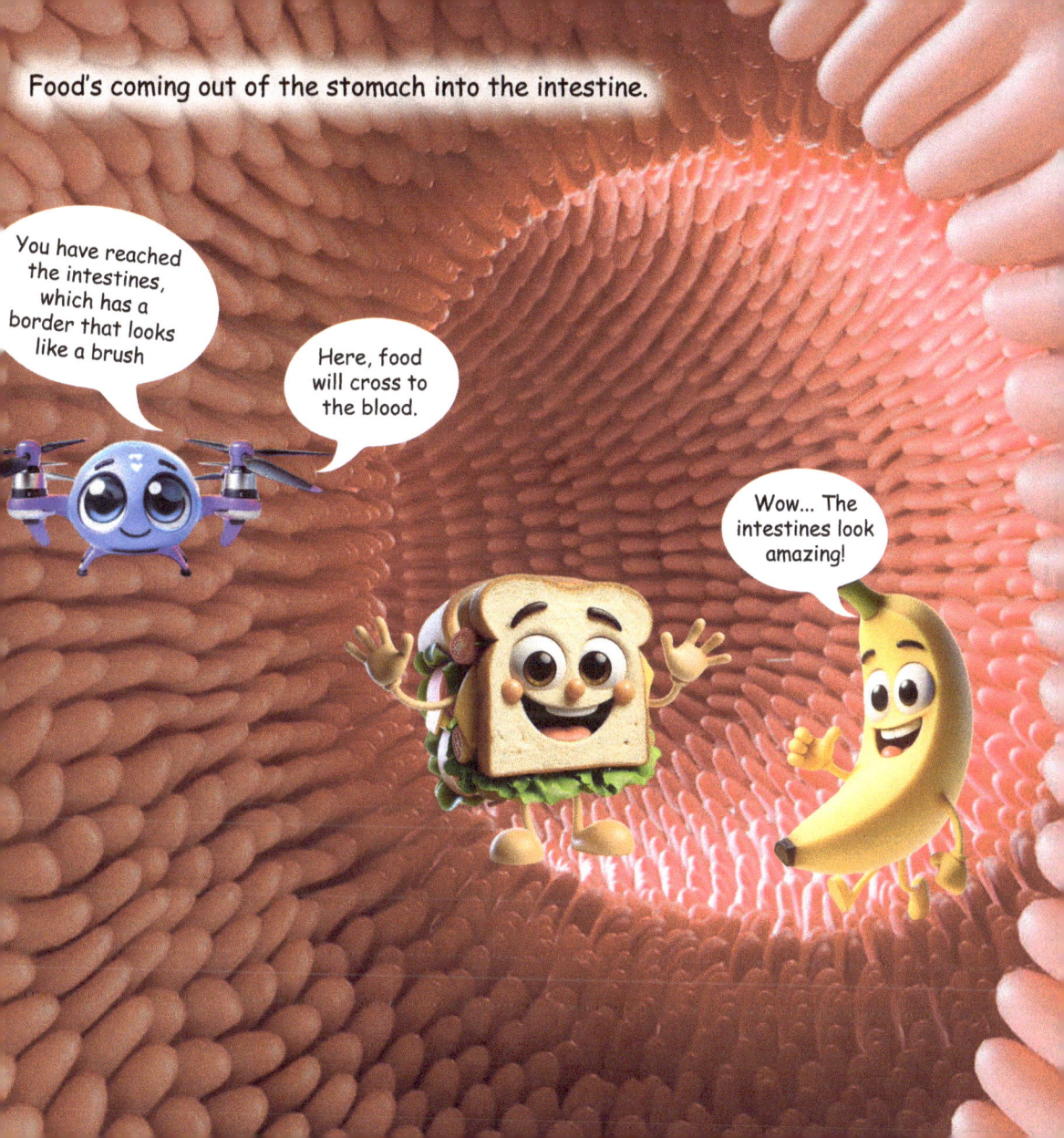

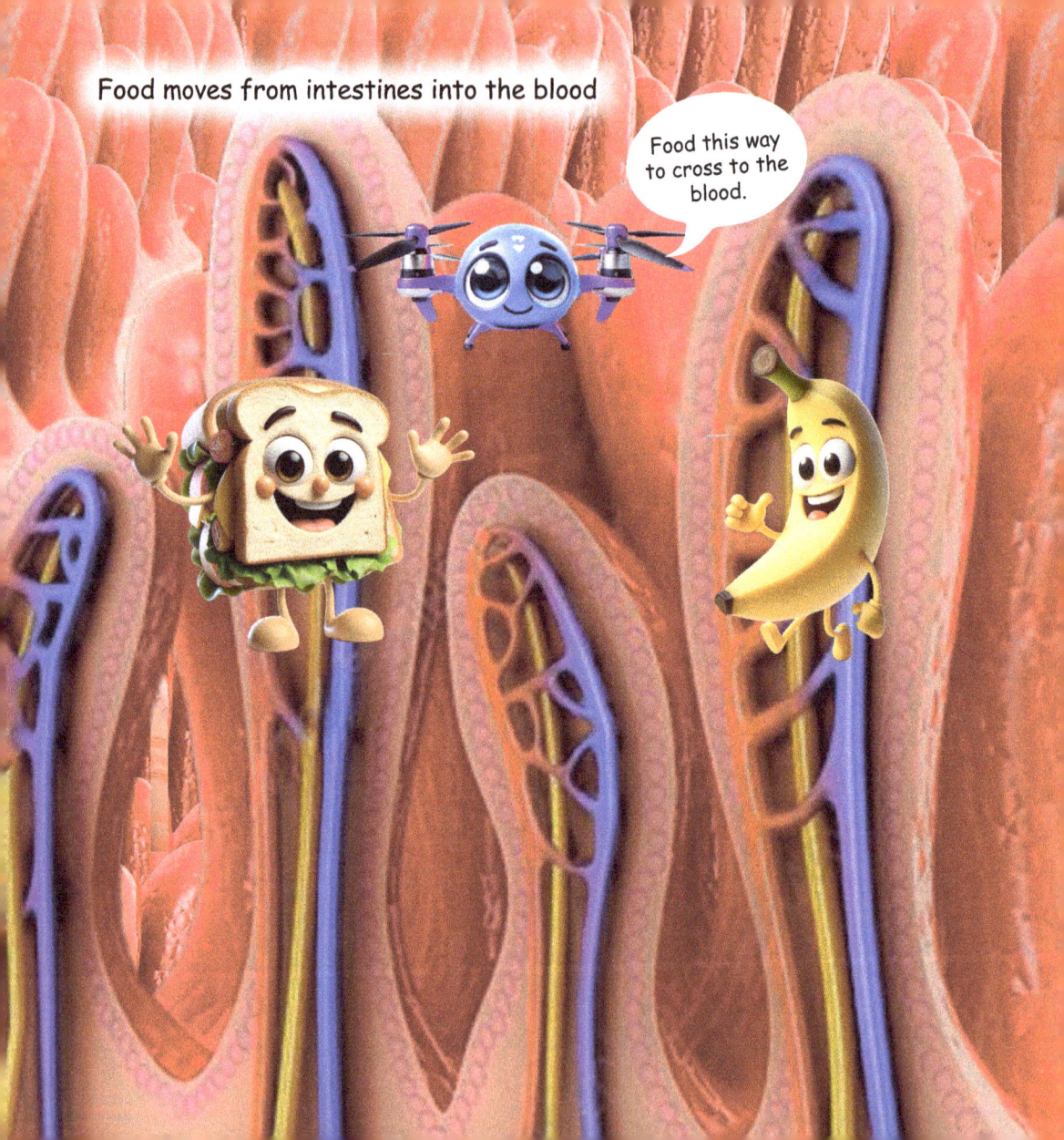

Ahmed went to his room to get some rest.

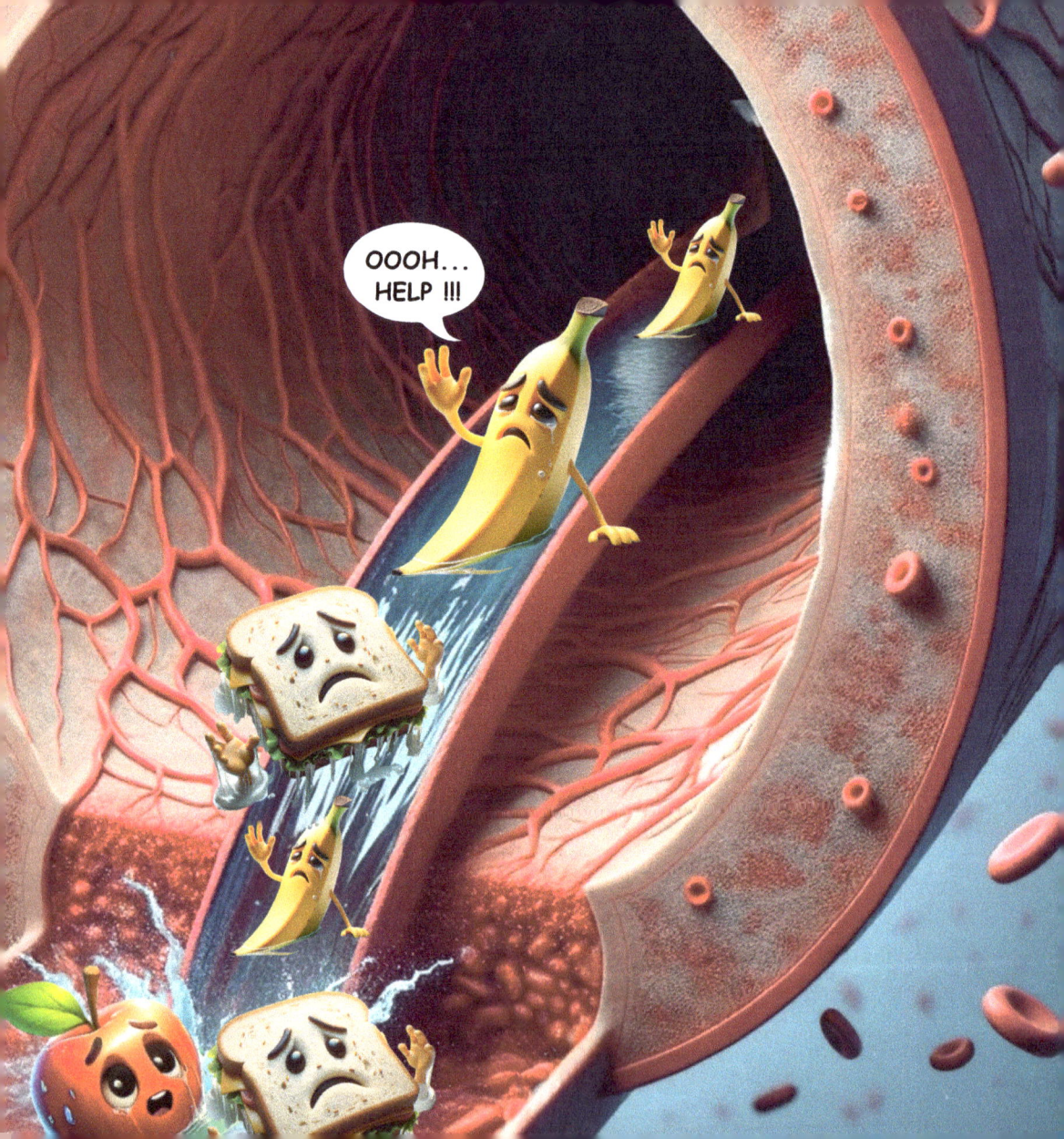

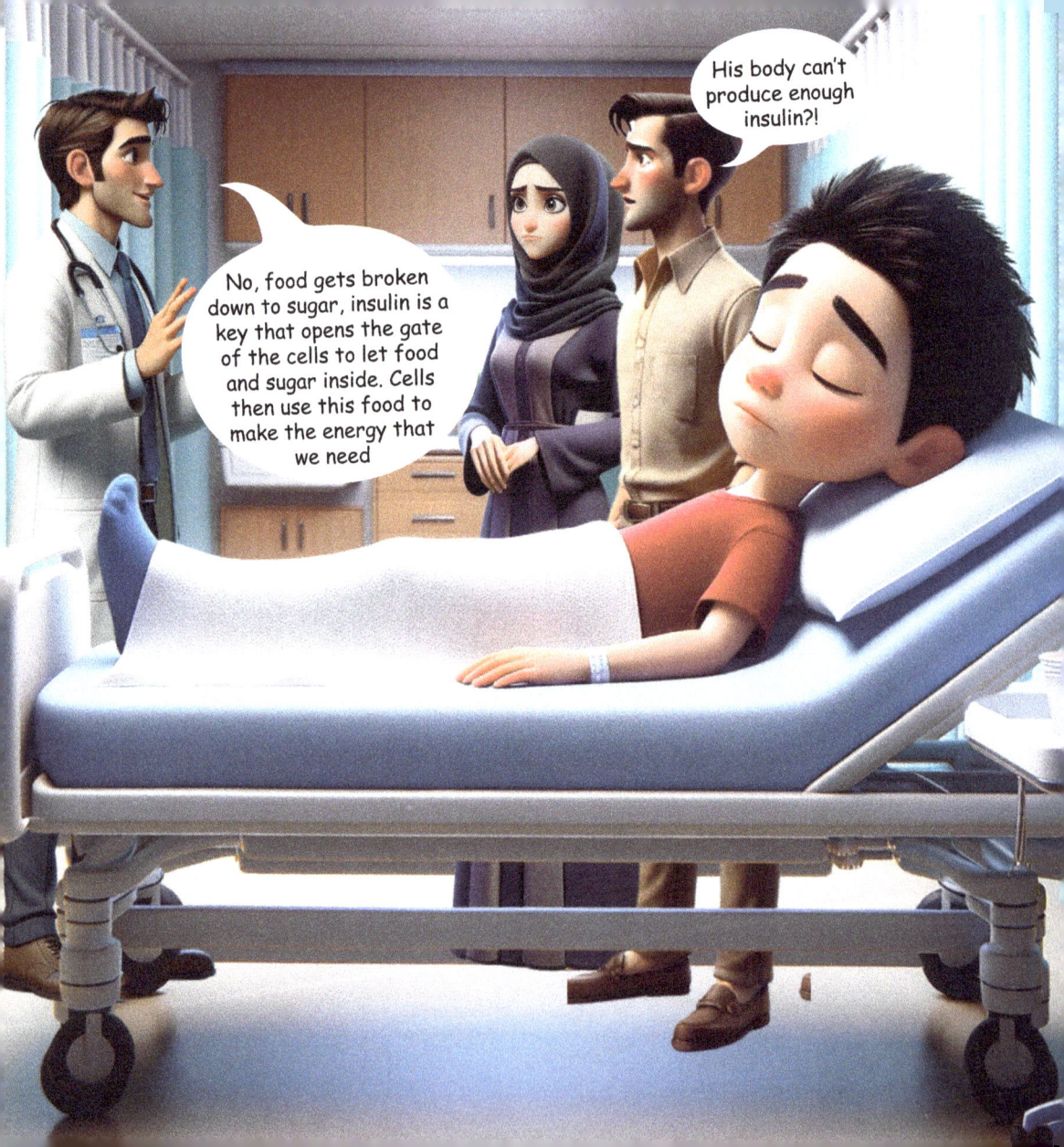

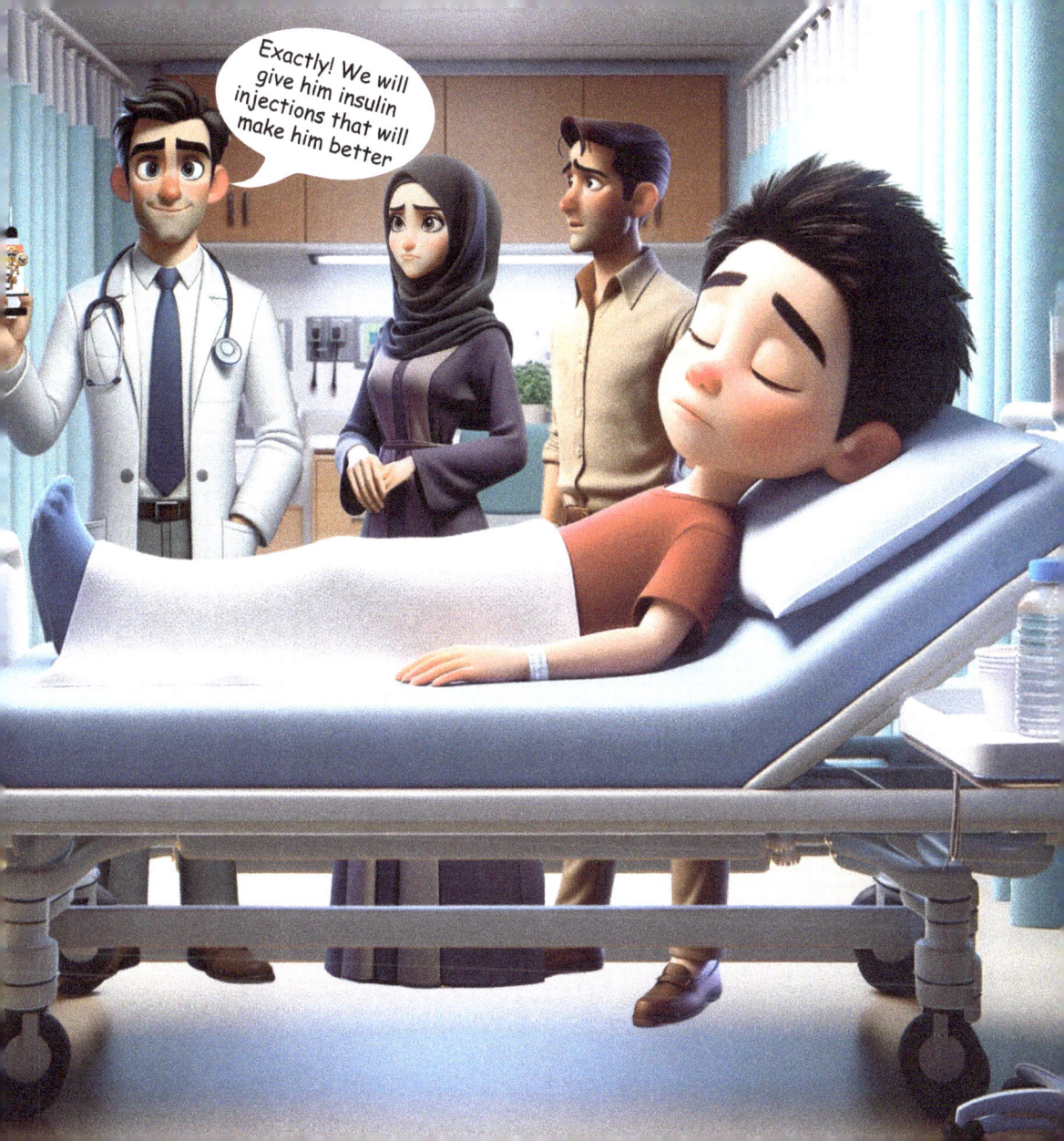

Hey kids!
We have a super fun survey for you and your parents!
It's all about understanding something cool called type 1 diabetes!
After you read an awesome story, your parents will ask you some questions.
Your answers will help us see how much you know about type 1 diabetes! then this QR code

Scan me!

Dear parents, we kindly request your participation in our survey to assess your child's understanding of type 1 diabetes after reading a children's story. Your input is valuable in helping us evaluate the effectiveness of our educational materials.

Thank you for taking the time to complete the survey!

Scan me!

About the Author

Dr. Dauleh is a physician, passionate about children's health education and storytelling. With a background in paediatric endocrinology and diabetology, Dr. Dauleh brings professional expertise and a personal commitment to helping children understand and manage their health.

Acknowledgments

I would like to express my heartfelt gratitude to my Pediatrics Endocrine team at Sidra Medicine, especially, Dr. Khalid Hussain, Dr. Goran Petroveski, and Judith Campbell, for their invaluable assistance in bringing the vision of this story to life. A special thank you to my mentors, family, and friends who tirelessly reviewed each version of the manuscript. Your support, insights, and encouragement were essential in making this book a reality.

www.ingramcontent.com/pod-product-compliance
Lightning Source LLC
LaVergne TN
LVHW072013060526
838200LV00059B/4667